MY FIRST MASS

Activity Book

For Catholic Kids

_____

IT'S TIME TO GO TO MASS!

Welcome to Church

Bless yourself with Holy Water

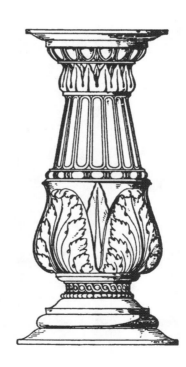

In the name of the

Father

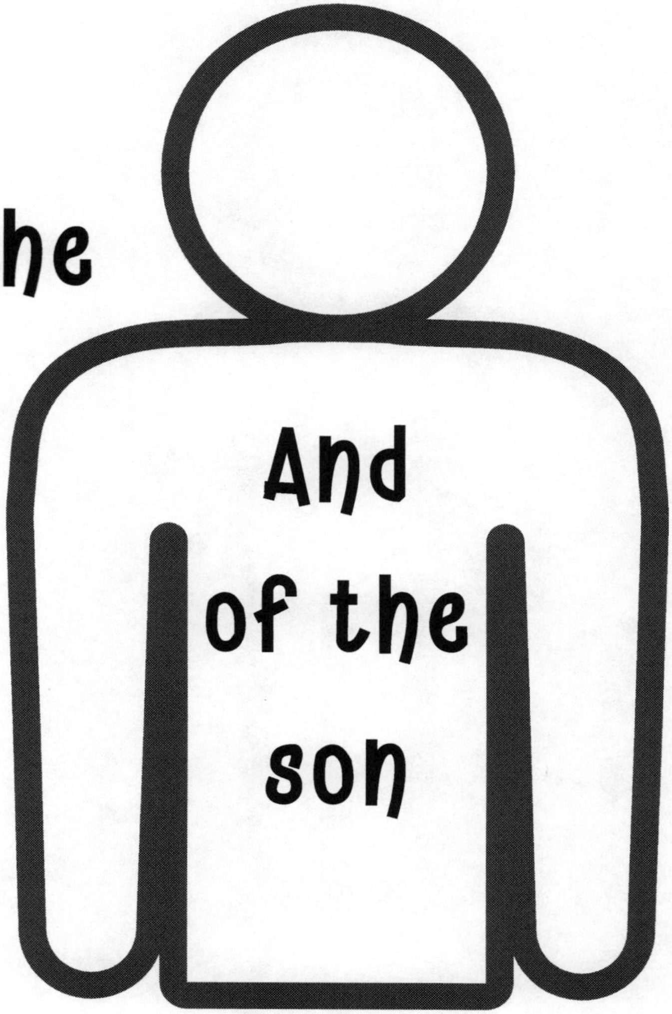

And of the

Spirit

Holy

And

of the

son

Please Stand

Watch the Procession

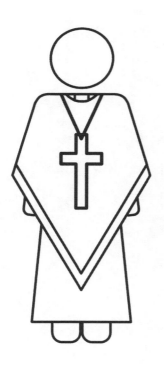

Time to Sit

Listen to the Readings

Reader: "The Word of the Lord"

You say:

THANKS BE TO GOD

Stand for the Gospel

Priest: The Lord be with you.

ALL: AND WITH YOUR SPIRIT.

Priest: A reading from the Holy Gospel according to... [Matthew, Mark, Luke, or John]

ALL: GLORY TO YOU, O LORD!

After the Gospel Proclamation:

Priest: The Gospel of the Lord.

ALL: PRAISE TO YOU, LORD JESUS CHRIST!

Sit and Listen to the Homily

Please Stand

The Creed and the
Prayer of the Faithful

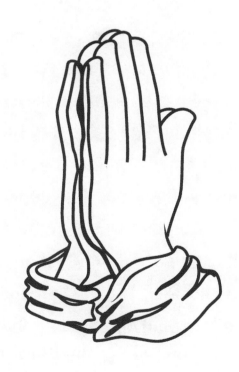

NICENO-CONSTANTINOPOLITAN CREED:

I believe in one God, the Father almighty, maker of heaven and earth, of all things visible and invisible.

I believe in one Lord Jesus Christ, the Only Begotten Son of God, born of the Father before all ages. God from God, Light from Light, true God from true God, begotten, not made, consubstantial with the Father; through him all things were made. For us men and for our salvation he came down from heaven,

[bow during the next two lines:]

and by the Holy Spirit was incarnate of the Virgin Mary, and became man. For our sake he was crucified under Pontius Pilate, he suffered death and was buried, and rose again on the third day in accordance with the Scriptures. He ascended into heaven and is seated at the right hand of the Father. He will come again in glory to judge the living and the dead and his kingdom will have no end.

I believe in the Holy Spirit, the Lord, the giver of life, who proceeds from the Father and the Son, who with the Father and the Son is adored and glorified, who has spoken through the prophets.

I believe in one, holy, catholic and apostolic Church. I confess one baptism for the forgiveness of sins and I look forward to the resurrection of the dead and the life of the world to come. Amen.

Sit for the Offertory

Find the Following Items

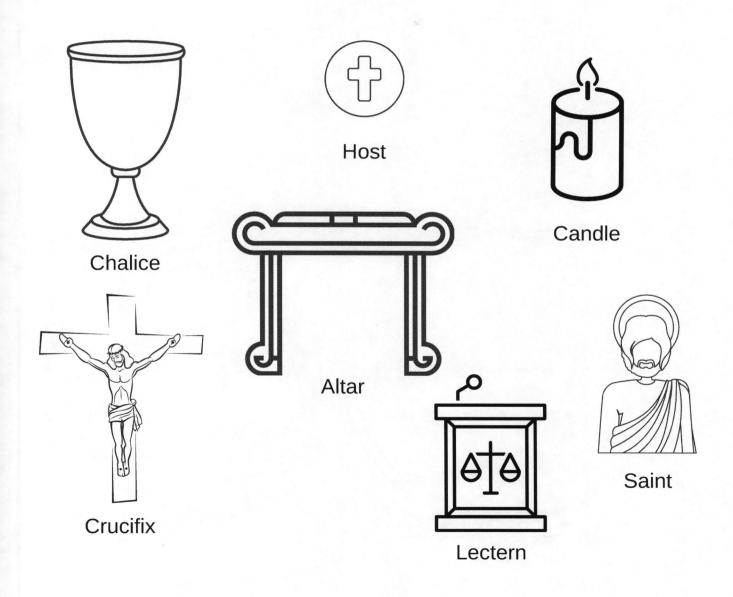

Chalice

Host

Candle

Altar

Crucifix

Lectern

Saint

The priest washes his hands

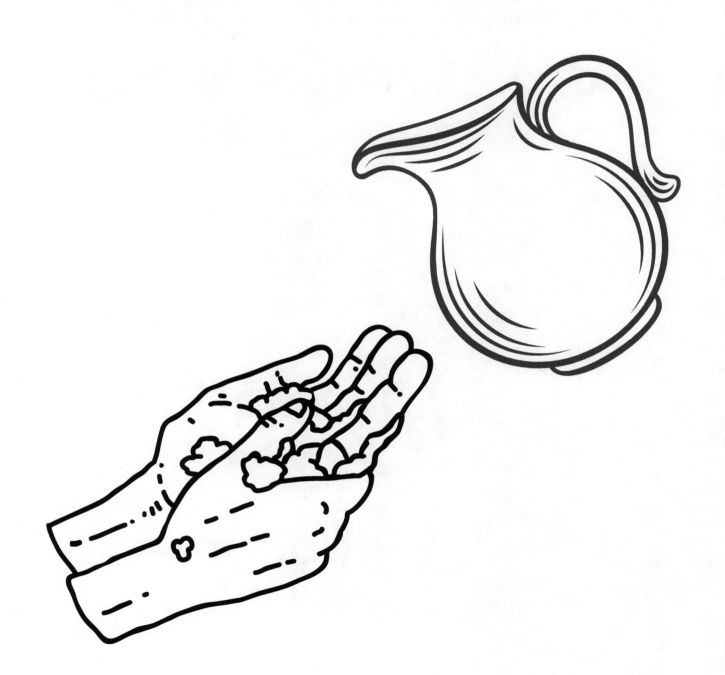

Stand for the Preface
(until the Holy Holy Holy)

Kneel for the Consecration

Stand After the Great Amen

The Lord's Prayer

OUR FATHER WHO ART IN HEAVEN,
HALLOWED BE THY NAME. THY
KINGDOM COME, THY WILL BE DONE,
ON EARTH AS IT IS IN HEAVEN.
GIVE US THIS DAY OUR DAILY
BREAD, AND FORGIVE US OUR
TRESPASSES, AS WE FORGIVE
THOSE WHO TRESPASS AGAINST
US. AND LEAD US NOT INTO
TEMPTATION, BUT DELIVER US
FROM EVIL. AMEN

The Sign of Peace

Shake hands, wave, or give peace sign

Kneel After the Lamb of God

Time For Communion

Kneel and pray after communion

Stand after Communion until the end of Mass

Closing Blessing

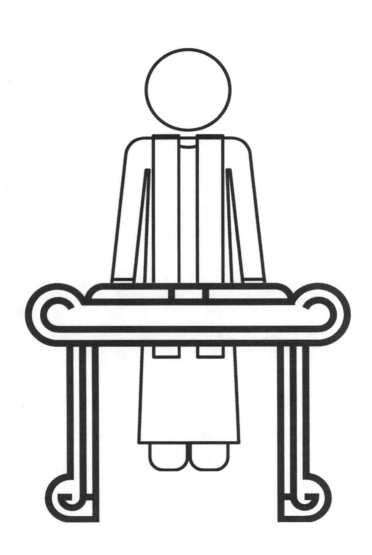

"Go forth, the Mass is ended."

You Say:

THANKS BE TO GOD

Watch the exit Procession

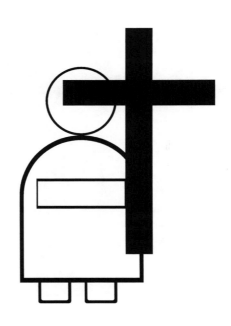

The Mass has ended, go in peace

Draw Your Favorite
Part of Mass

Made in United States
Troutdale, OR
04/15/2024